Credit Help For Millennials

"Your Guide to Navigating This Everchanging World"

J.E Lewis III

Cover design by: J.E Lewis III
Printed in the United States of America

I dedicate this work to my Mother, without her none of this would be feasible.

Prologue

From Elementary to Highschool we were taught everything from memorizing the periodic table to longhand trigonometry. We were taught how to "Please excuse our dear Aunt Sally" and sadly as we've grown up Aunt Sally and we have become distant relatives. The general consensus in Millenials is that we were taught a lot of useless things in school that holds no value in our day to day lives. Not once after high school have I had to use the Pythagoras Theory, make dioramas, or navigate the Encyclopedia Brittanica. If the previous items I mentioned are completely oblivious to you then my point has been proven. I rest my case.

Chapter 1

What is Credit?

Credit is the ability of a customer to receive a good or service with the understanding they will pay later. So for example, anytime you see a furniture store saying "buy here, pay here" they are offering credit. You want that new IPhone 11 Pro Max but don't have $1249, you can use credit to pay off the phone monthly, this is a normal practice for cell phone companies. Whenever you apply for credit the lenders are calculating if based on the information provided you can be trusted to pay back the amount owed and any interest charges. This is the same regardless of the merchant/lender you are trying to get a loan, goods, or services from.

There are four types of credit, revolving credit, charge cards, service credit, and installment credit. With **revolving credit** you are given a limit that you can use up to that limit. You must make a minimum payment each month which is set by the lender. Whatever balance you have after making your payment you will carry over to your next month. The most common form of revolving credit is a credit card. **Charge cards** are rarely used today but work pretty much like credit cards but you must pay the full balance by the end of the month. The next form of credit is **service credit** which is arguably the first type of credit most people establish. These companies will allow you to use their service under the assumption that you will pay at a later date. This is the credit that cell phone companies give you when you are establishing a phone line. The last form of credit is installment billing. **Installment billing** is a loan for a specific amount of money that you agree to pay back. Examples of this would be car loans and mortgages. If you get a $100,000 house and pay for it over 30 years you would pay $277 not counting interest. This is installment billing. You may ask "why do I need credit?". I'll tell you the main reasons you need it. Credit is a tool that you can use to help you buy things you need now but pay for them over time. So unless you are apart of the 3% of people that can buy a home cash, you need credit. Good credit is also needed for other things such as better interest rates and better terms on whatever you are financing. These examples are things that you would encounter only if you decide. Some people never even buy their own home or finance anything. There are other examples for you as well. Most landlords check your credit when you are applying for an apartment. Insurance companies also check your credit when deciding if they are going to cover you. Even certain jobs will turn you away if you have delinquent or nonexistent credit. I say that to say this, YOU CAN'T DO ANYTHING WITHOUT CREDIT.

Chapter 2

Building credit

Do I still have your attention? Ok, enough rambling about how much you need credit. Now I'll show you ways to actually build that credit. Credit is weird in a few ways. Certain places won't give you credit if you don't have credit. Which leads someone looking to establish credit scratching their head. How can I get credit if I've never had credit? I'm glad you asked. There are a few ways to get started. Establishing credit seems like rocket science but once you get that first credit account it opens up doors for other opportunities.

The first and easiest way to establish credit is by applying for a credit card. Most banks will give you a credit card to help you establish credit even if you don't have credit. Credit Unions are normally the best option if you plan on taking this route. Credit unions have fixed interest rates on mostly any form of credit they offer, this is because credit unions are nonprofits. Most credit unions require you to work for the State or county you reside or be immediate family to someone that has an account already. Once you have your account up and running after about three months you can go inside and apply for a credit card. They will most likely ask for your most recent paystub, the reason you want a credit card and lastly they will run your credit. If you get approved they will send you a card within a week. Being that you have little to no credit they will approve you for anything in between $250 to $500 normally. Depending on the amount you make per month the credit limit can be drastically higher or lower.

If for some reason you can't get approved for the card you can apply for a secured credit card from. The difference between a credit card from a credit union and a secured credit card is with the secured credit card you have to pay a deposit. This deposit equals your credit limit. Creditors will use this practice to limit their risk. For example, if you don't pay they can take the money from your deposit. This is one of the easiest cards to be approved for because of the low risk to the creditor. One downfall of the secured card versus the credit card is the secured card has a significantly higher interest rate than the credit card. If you do opt for a secured card, First Premier Bank offers one with a $300 deposit that is designed for credit building/repair.

Another credit building account that I can personally vouch for is an app called Self. Self allows you to save money and build credit at the same time. Every time you make a payment it will show positive payment history on your credit. You will create an account and decide how long you want to pay into the savings account. You have two options, you can pay $25 a month for 24 months or $45 a month for 12months. Once the term has ended Self will direct deposit that money back to the account of your choosing. It's honestly that simple. If you go the 24-month route then at the end of the term you will receive six hundred dollars back. If you go the 12-month route you will receive $545 back. Self will report to your credit within the first three months, this account will help your credit in multiple ways. It will show "on-time payments" and positive credit history to all three credit bureaus.

Another great feature that Self recently rolled out is a secured credit card. The great thing about this card is that you can take the money that you save into the Self account and use it as your credit limit. For example, if you save $200 you will be given the option in the app to use that amount towards your credit limit. There are hundreds of options to build your credit, you must do your due diligence when analyzing other credit building techniques.

Credit-builder loans are another great option when trying to establish credit. They are exactly what they sound like, loans designed to build credit. This is like a forced savings account. Typically the money you borrow for the loan is held in a savings account until it is paid back. The payments you make towards the loan are reported each month until the loan is paid back. This loan is not offered by all banks, it is normally offered by credit unions and community banks.

Payday loans are another good option if your bank offers them. Don't get frightened because you see the term "payday loan". This isn't the same type of loan that comes on at 3 a.m that has you paying an arm and a leg just to try and make ends meet. Banks normally won't even call them a payday loan, they use terms like "salary advance" and or "loan advance". Credit unions are another great option when using this method. Payday loans are exactly what they sound like, a loan you get until payday. Certain banks do up to $500 and they normally want to set up the money to autodraft out of your bank account the day you get paid. The great thing about getting them through your bank is that they report to your credit every month even on the months you don't use it. For example, John gets paid every other Friday, he borrows $400 the day after he gets paid to pay an unexpected bill that he didn't calculate into his budget. John's bank will expect that money back on his next payday which is two weeks away. When that day comes they will auto-draft that money out of his account plus interest. The interest will vary depending on your bank. Once John's payment successfully goes through the bank will report to his credit, on-time payments.

Becoming an authorized user on a credit card account can have a significant impact on your credit. The easiest way to become an authorized user is to have a family member or significant other add you to his or her credit card account. Doing so adds that card's payment history to your credit. You will want to use someone who has a good and long credit history especially with the card that you will be added to. You don't have to possess the card or use it at all. You should however ensure before getting added to the card that you can trust this person to do the right thing when it pertains to their own credit and that card. The amount of points that this method can improve your credit varies based on your credit. For example, if you become an authorized user on an account that has an age of 10+ years and your average age of credit is 1 year then this will boost your credit dramatically. On the other hand, if your credit age is 9 years already then you may not see a significant boost in that area but you could see a boost in others such as a lower utilization rate and on-time payment history just to name a few.

Chapter 3

Credit Report

We've knocked out "what is credit" and "ways to build credit". You should now be well educated on how to integrate credit into your life. Now I want to go over how your credit report is broken down. As stated previously whenever you attempt to apply for credit the creditors will pull your credit report. Your credit holds multiple factors that the creditors take into consideration. On the next page is a breakdown of the factors and how much they are weighted on your report to make up your credit score.

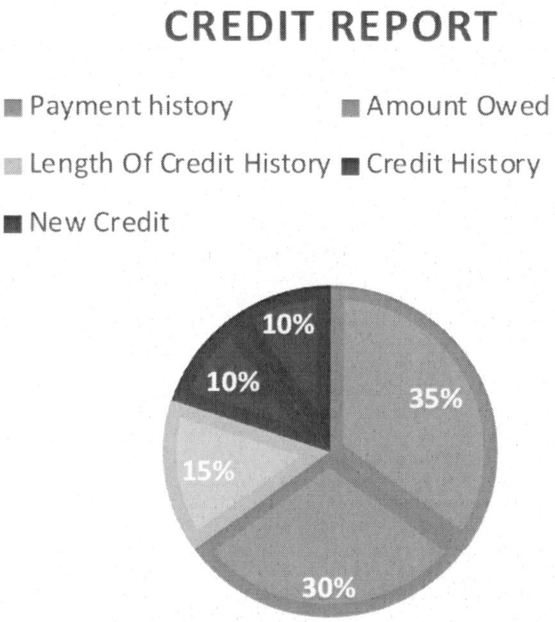

Payment history is the biggest factor and rightfully so, regardless of what form of credit you have, you must make payments on time. Missing or being late on one payment can drop your score up to 100 points. The amount owed section includes the balance you have on your credit cards or loans. Everything from house loans to car loans and personal loans shows up in this section. Length of credit history is a little tricky and may be one of the hardest aspects of the credit score to maintain when first trying to build credit. This is because to build credit you must add more credit accounts but each time you add one the average

age of your credit account drops. Length of credit also applies to the overall age of your credit accounts. Credit mix refers to the different accounts that make up your credit report. This could include, student loans, mortgages, credit cards, personal loans, etc. Lastly, there is new credit which negatively affects your credit score when you get new credit, it could be anything from a delinquent hospital bill or applying for a credit card. This puts a hard inquiry on your credit which lasts for 2 years. A hard inquiry can reduce your credit by 5 to 10 points.

Understanding your credit report is critical to your overall credit building. There are three credit bureaus, Equifax, TransUnion, and Experian. Credit bureaus maintain your credit information. Depending on where you establish credit, everyone may not report to every credit bureau. This is also true when creditors pull your credit to make a decision, they may pull all three credit bureaus or sometimes just one. For example, my credit union only reports to Equifax every month, but my Self Lender account reports to all three credit bureaus. This is why if you ever monitor your credit reports all three will normally be different. When dealing with major creditors such as Discover or Capital One they normally pull from your Experian but also weigh your score from the other two bureaus. Your credit report includes the number of credit accounts you have, the number of loans you've taken out, and how much you've paid back, it also includes your payment history whether you pay on time or have late or missed payments. Lastly, it includes collection and negative accounts. The most common collection account that most people have on their report is hospital bills. Accounts go to collections after not being paid. The time it takes varies depending on where you are located and the type of credit that is going to collections. To avoid an account going to collections, pay on time, and maintain communication with creditors. What's a good credit score? Of course everyone wants the very best credit score possible which is an 850. This takes time and patience. Your credit score has a range. These ranges determine whether your credit is poor, fair, good, very good, or excellent. Your credit can be anywhere from 300-850.

Poor Credit: 300-579
Fair Credit:580-669
Good Credit:670-739
Very Good Credit:740-799
Excellent Credit:800-850
These numbers vary based on the scale they are measured on.

Chapter 4

Maintaining Credit

Your score fluctuates from time to time for a variety of reasons. You can control the majority of the reasons your score fluctuates by making smart credit decisions. For example, credit utilization is something that can make or break your score. The higher the utilization the more your score will drop. Credit utilization in lay terms is simply how much of your available credit you have used. This doesn't apply to certain forms of credit like installment or service credit. It applies to things like credit cards and credit lines. The general rule of thumb is to stay below 30% utilization. So, for example, John has a credit card with a $10,000 limit, he runs his balance up to $5,000. This puts him at 50% utilization because he is using half of his credit limit. Utilization is calculated based on the total balance of your total credit limit. This means that it includes all your available credit, whether you have 1 card or 5. If you have multiple cards the easiest way to calculate your utilization is: Total Balance / Total Credit Limit=Credit Utilization X 100=Utilization(percent) As previously stated in chapter 3 the "amount owed" section of your credit accounts for 30% of your overall score and credit utilization is one the most important factors that make up that section. Age of credit is another important factor when it comes to maintaining credit. A long history of credit shows you have more experience using credit. Anytime you get a new account on your credit it will begin tracking the length that you've had it. With credit the main thing to remember is DON'T CLOSE ACCOUNTS. Sometimes this will be out of your control, especially with things like personal loans because the loans are given to you based on terms which include the amount of time you have to pay the money back. Once that money is paid back the account will close. It will close in "Good Standing" as long as it's paid back in full and on time but the fact remains is that it will close. I've had accounts close that led to my credit dropping anywhere from 20-35 points. If at all possible you don't want to close any account. Things like credit cards and credit lines are good forms of revolving credit. Accounts like these two forms will report good standing every month which will also simultaneously increase your age of credit.

Disputing accounts is a must when it comes to maintaining credit. Creditors will sometimes add accounts to your credit that are inaccurate. These accounts could be inaccurate in a few ways, the amount owed may be incorrect, or the account could be someone else debt. Disputing an account is pretty simple. You can either call the credit bureau or visit their website and submit a dispute. If you decide to call the credit bureau, you will have to speak with an individual and tell them which account you are disputing and why. They will submit your dispute and contact the creditor, the creditor will have 30 days to reply. The creditors will receive the dispute and will either accept or deny the claim. If they accept that the information is true then the incorrect account will be removed from your credit. If they deny your claim then the account will stay on your credit, for now. If the creditor doesn't reply then the account must come off. This process is pretty much the same when disputing online except for online you can add proof of your claim such as documents showing the account has been paid or closed. The great thing about disputing accounts is that you can submit disputes as many times as you like. If for some reason the creditor doesn't reply within those 30 days the account will come off. This is what those "credit repair" companies do. You can do this same thing yourself and protect your wallet at the same time. I used this same method when disputing a $1200 collection account I received from an insurance company. I disputed the account over the phone first, the company replied to the credit bureau and told them the account was accurate. I disputed the account again but the second time I used the Equifax online portal and uploaded my bill and documents showing that number was incorrect. Within 30 days the account was removed and my score increased 45 points. I repeated this same process for TransUnion. Different creditors report to different credit bureaus, my incorrect account was only reported to Equifax and Transunion, therefore, I only had to dispute on those two. I will place the websites and phone numbers for each credit bureau at the end of the book so you can get the ball rolling.

Chapter 5

Credit Monitoring

Simply put credit monitoring allows you to monitor your credit. It allows you to track changes in your score or credit report. Different credit monitoring apps all relatively function the same way, with some having certain exclusive features. Credit monitoring apps give you a breakdown of your score, tips to improve your score, and some even offer home loan calculators, which would have you input your information and generate you a rough estimate of your home buying power. I've used a few. Here are the ones I like the most.

Credit Karma

This is the main one I use daily, in my opinion, I believe this is the best credit monitoring app for a few reasons. Credit Karma allows you to view "offers". In the "offers" section is multiple credit cards or personal loans from multiple creditors. The good thing about Credit Karma is that they show you your approval odds for the particular offer. The higher the percentage the higher the chance of your being approved. Credit Karma also has a home buying simulator that you can input information into. It is normally information such as your savings account amount, your monthly income, your monthly debt, and of course your credit score. The simulator will instantly give you an amount, this is your home buying power. Credit Karma also lets you monitor 2 of the 3 credit bureaus. The two that it allows you to monitor are Equifax and Transunion. On both reports you will be able to see the payment history, credit card utilization, derogatory marks, age of credit, hard inquires, and total accounts. Credit Karma also allows you to dispute incorrect items directly from the app. Credit Karma offers plenty of other features, from filing your taxes to monthly credit coaching. One final thing to note is that Credit Karma displays a Vantage 3.0 credit scoring system as opposed to the FICO credit score system. This will explain why when you view your score on another credit monitoring platform it displays two different numbers.

Experian

Another credit monitoring app I like is the Experian app. Experian is one of the three major credit bureaus and has a lot of great features as well. Similar to the Credit Karma app, the Experian app recommends credit cards to you and displays your chances of being approved. It also has a portal that shows your chances of getting approved for a personal loan. Unlike Credit Karma, Experian allows you to monitor all three credit bureaus. Arguably the best feature of the Experian app is the ”Experian Boost feature. This feature can instantly boost your Experian score for free. This feature can give you credit history for payments you've made ok things that never reported to your credit. The three options that it currently offers is your electric bill, your phone bill, and your water bill. Experian will go back up to 2 years and give you full credit on your report. This means you will get two years of on-time payment history, among other things reported to your credit.

Mint Money Manager

Mint is another credit monitoring app I've used in the past. It is similar to Credit Karma and Experian. Mint Mobile monitors your credit score and gives tips on how to improve your credit score. My favorite feature from Mint is it allows you to connect investment accounts, credit cards, and bank accounts. This is extremely useful for someone who is into stock trading among other things. This feature is what sets Mint apart from others because it provides you a complete overview of all your finances in one place.

Scenario 1

Car Buying

When you are buying a car you have a few options, the method you use to get the car should be as efficient as possible. The first thing I would do first is to find out if you're eligible for a car loan through your bank, this saves you a lot of trouble and your credit score will thank you. The reason I say your credit score will thank you is because when you go into a car lot and try to get financing you have to worry about them "shotgunning" your credit. When a car lot is having trouble getting you financed they will send your credit application to multiple lenders hoping that someone will accept it. It may seem like they are working "really hard" to get a deal done but in reality for every lender that they send your application to an inquiry is placed on your credit report that can decrease your credit anywhere from 2-10 points per account. So if they send your application to 5 lenders you are looking at anywhere from a 10-50 point decrease. This 10-50 point decrease will last for two years. Shotgunning doesn't happen to every person and it may not happen to you, but if you have subpar credit 9 times out of 10 you will experience it. One easy way to avoid this practice is to get an auto loan from your bank. Normally what you will need are two pay stubs to prove income, demographic information(address, social security number, current employer, length of employment), residence status, and the amount of your monthly rent/housing payment(if applicable). Lastly, you will also be asked about the number of dependents you have such as a child or sick parent, and if you pay child support or alimony. Once you have this information you can either head directly to where you bank at or you can call the after-hours line and do the application over the phone with a 24-hour agent (not all banks may offer this feature). If you decide to go the route of going inside the branch location you should ask to speak with a loan officer, once you are checked in someone will come out to greet and take you in the back. At that time you inform them that you would like to apply for an auto loan, give them your information, they will run your credit and give you a decision normally within 10 mins. If you are approved they will give you a max limit, this limit becomes your car buying power. This simply is the max amount the lender will loan you. While at the bank they should already go over your interest rate. Your bank will give you the monthly payment amount once you decide on a car. Now comes the fun part, deciding what car you want. Travel to a car lot and decide which car you want. NEVER take the first offer they give you on the car you want, do your research on the car, and find out what's a reasonable price for the car. Once you decide on the car let the dealership know you have your own financing call your bank and have them fax over your paperwork directly to the dealership. The dealership will go over the warranty information, some cars will come with a warranty, if not the decision to purchase the warranty is up to you. Purchasing this car will build positive credit history every month in multiple ways from on-time payments to age of credit. Disclaimer: Your car-buying situation and interaction may vary from this one.

Scenario 2

Purchasing a Home

Just like any other purchase you want to make sure your credit is at least a decent score before you apply for a home loan. The higher the credit score, the lower the interest rate. One of the best routes to go for people who don't make a significant amount of money would be to apply for an FHA loan. FHA loans are designed for people with low to moderate-income. They are issued by an FHA approved lender and insured by the Federal Housing Administration. The reason this is a great option is that FHA loans require lower down payments and lower credit scores. As of 2020, you can borrow up to 96.5% of the value of a home. This will leave you to pay only 3.5% down. So for example, if you are looking at purchasing an $80,000 house you only need to make a down payment of $2,800. Sounds good right? That's cause it is. Now back to the credit score. To get an FHA you need only a minimum credit score of 580. Other things come into play such as things you have on your credit. You may have a 580 but if you have a major collection account on your credit then you would need to take care of that account first in most situations. The situation varies per person. This is also true when it comes to having a 580 credit score to apply, people have applied with less and have been approved. Multiple banks offer this type of loan and many more. They each have positive and negative things about them. Weigh your options. After getting approved for your loan you must pick out a home. Try to get something that is in your budget. The general rule of thumb when purchasing a home is that you can afford a mortgage 2 to 2.5 times your annual income. For example, If you make $60,000 annually you can purchase a home that is up to $150,000. Based on your credit score and down payment your home buying power will increase. Lastly, an FHA loan requires you to pay two types of mortgage insurance, UFMIP, and MIP. The Upfront Mortage Insurance Premium is equal to 1.75% of the base loan. This is paid at the time of your closing or it can be rolled into the loan. The Annual Mortgage Insurance Premium is paid monthly and is normally a percentage of the base loan amount. This scenario is for people who use FHA loans. There are plenty of other loan types out there and everyone's process is different. This should get you started in the right direction.

Parting Words

You've got this! Apply all of the previous steps and the sky is the limit. I have personally used all of the steps that are in this book. You should be well versed in starting your credit repair/building journey now. If you are trying to establish credit, get a secured card. If you are trying to rebuild your credit, evaluate it, and begin disputing accounts. When attempting to maintain your credit, pay your bills on time, keep a low utilization rate, don't close credit cards, and limit your applications for new forms of credit. Everything is a stepping stone, be patient, and apply your newfound knowledge. I'm rooting for you!

Credit Terminology

Billing Cycle-The number of days between statements. This varies per credit account, normally it can be anywhere from 30-45 days. Easily explained it is the time in between your bill.

Interest Rate-The percentage that a creditor charges for lending money. Varies based on credit.

Minimum Amount Due-This is the lowest amount that needs to be paid to keep an account in good standing.

Annual Percentage Rate (APR)-Annual Rate that takes interest and fees into account. This varies per account and is a percentage.

Payoff Amount-Total dollar amount that must be paid to close out an account. Down Payment-One-time payment that is paid upfront. Common when purchasing a car or home. Down payments greatly improve your odds of getting approved for a loan.

Cosigner-Person who signs a credit or loan application along with the primary borrower. A cosigner strengthens your chances of being approved. If approved the cosigner becomes equally responsible for repaying the debt.

Credit Bureau Contact Information

Ai.equifax.com/CreditInvestigation

1-800-685-1111

Experian.com/disputes/main.html

1-888-397-3742

Transunion.com/credit-disputes/dispute-your-credit 1-888-909-8872

Afterword

My experiences building my credit inspired me to write this book. I've gone through every emotion when it pertains to establishing/maintaining credit. Like most, I was never informed of the importance of credit until I decided to research it myself. By this time I had a few collection accounts totaling $3000, this forced me to educate myself on the most efficient techniques to rebuild my credit. I was able to dispute my collection accounts and successfully had them removed. Once removed I began adding various credit accounts that helped me diversify and build my credit report, this led to a 180 point credit increase in a short amount of time. Since then I've constantly increased my credit score and have been approved for different forms of credit that I could have never dreamed of. This inspired me to share my knowledge because I know many people will go through things in life that will lead them down the same path I once was.

About The Author

•

J.E Lewis III is currently an undergraduate student at East Carolina University working on his second degree. He is well versed in a few different areas but has a passion for business and financial literacy.

Made in United States
North Haven, CT
04 November 2026

21771224R00023